Joseph Haydn

Complete London Symphonies
in Full Score

EDITED BY

Ernst Praetorius

AND

H. C. Robbins Landon

SERIES II
Nos. 99–104

DOVER PUBLICATIONS, INC.
New York

This Dover edition, first published in 1985, is an unabridged republication of the music from six separate symphony volumes (Nos. 99–104) as published by Ernst Eulenburg Ltd., London (n. d.; publication numbers 431, 434, 439, 438, 469 and 409, respectively, of the Edition Eulenburg, or Eulenburg Miniature Scores). No. 100 was edited by H. C. Robbins Landon, the others by Ernst Praetorius.

Manufactured in the United States of America
Dover Publications, Inc., 31 East 2nd Street, Mineola, N.Y. 11501

Library of Congress Cataloging-in-Publication Data

Haydn, Joseph, 1732–1809.
  [Symphonies, H. I. 93–104]
  Complete London symphonies.

  Reprint. Originally published: London : E. Eulenburg.
  Contents: Ser. 1. Nos. 93–98—Ser. 2. Nos. 99–104.
  1. Symphonies—Scores. I. Praetorius, Ernst, 1880–   . II. Landon, H. C. Robbins
(Howard Chandler Robbins), 1926–   III. Title. IV. Title: London symphonies.
M1001.H4H.I,93–104   1985   85-752723
ISBN 0-486-24982-4 (pbk. : ser. 1)
ISBN 0-486-24983-2 (pbk. : ser. 2)

CONTENTS

NOTE: Editorial additions of dynamics, phrasing and the like appear within brackets.

Symphony No. 99 in E-flat Major

I

II

III

Menuetto. Allegretto

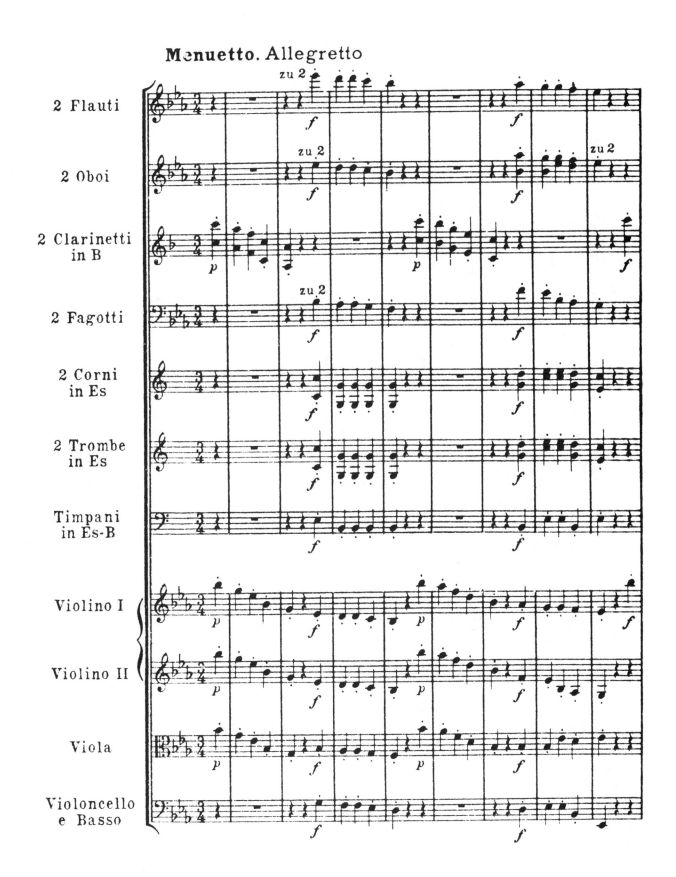

IV

Finale
Vivace

Symphony No. 100 in G Major ("Military")

III

IV

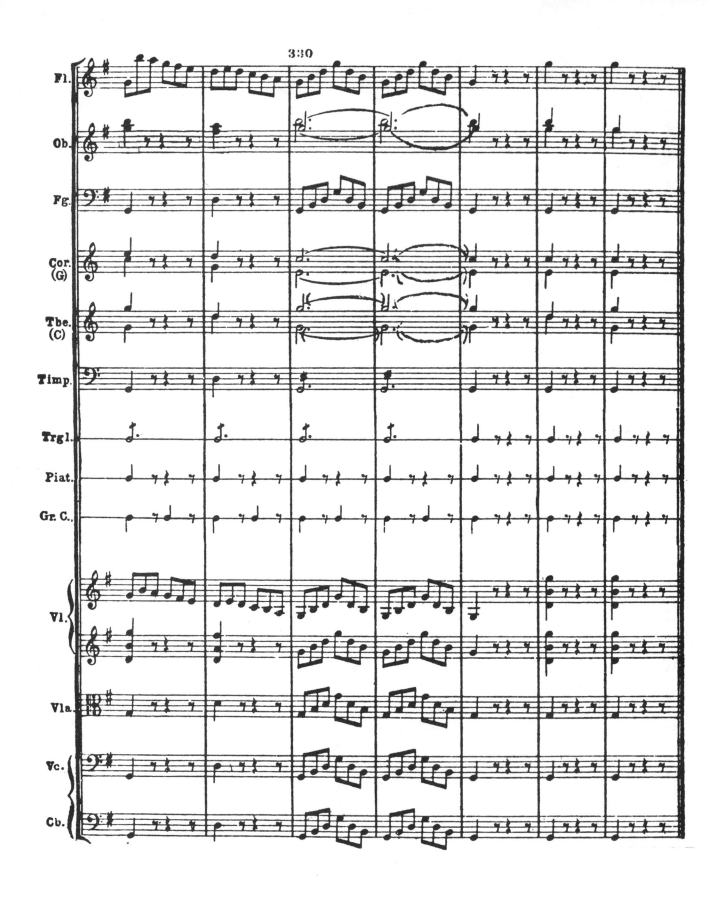

330

Symphony No. 101 in D Major ("The Clock")

I

*A part for clarinets is customarily given, although none appears in the autograph score.

II

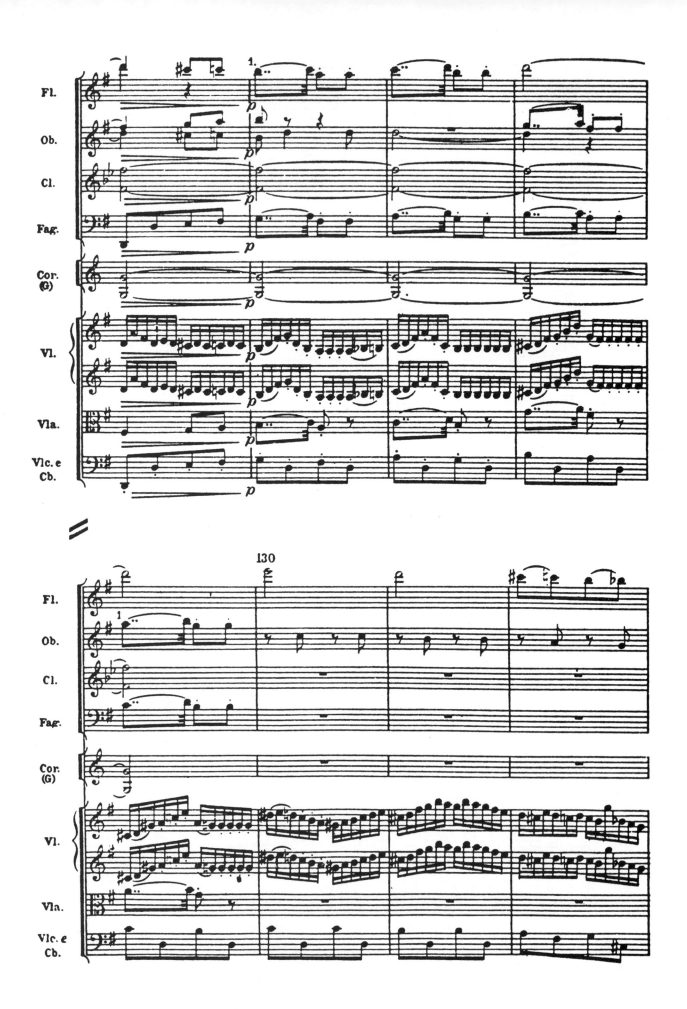

III

Menuetto. Allegretto

IV

Finale. Vivace

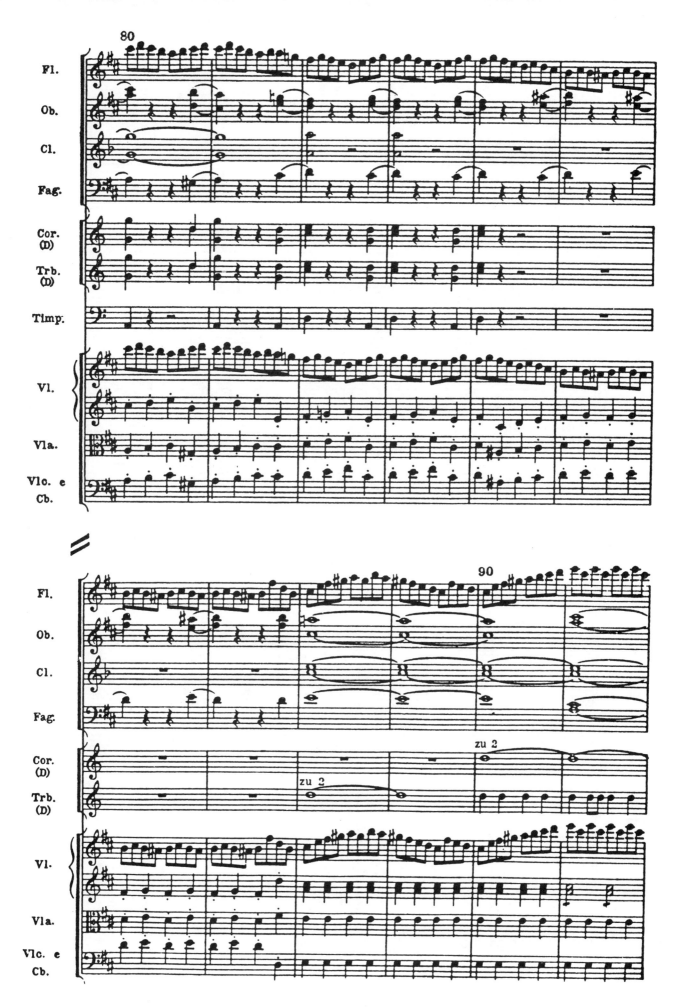

Symphony No. 102 in B-flat Major

I

Allegro vivace.

II

Adagio

IV

Symphony No. 103 in E-flat Major ("Drumroll")

I

Allegro con spirito
210
Fl.
Ob.
a 2
Cl.
a 2
Fag.
Cor. (Es)
a 2
Tr. (Es)
Timp.
Vl.
Vla.
Bassi
Vc. e B.
Vc.

based on 1st Vbr.

220

a 2

II
Andante più tosto Allegretto

Symphony No. 104 in D Major ("London")

I

II

Flauti

Oboi

★Clarinetti in A

Fagotti

Corni in G

Trombe in D

Timpani in D-A

Violino I

Violino II

Viola

Violoncello e Contrabasso

Vl.

Vla.

Vc. e Cb.

Vc.

Bassi

★A part for clarinets is customarily given, although none appears in movements II–IV of the autograph score.

III

Menuetto Allegro

IV

Finale: Spiritoso